MW01674990

H

The Ultimate Guide to Anger Management, Discover Expert Tips and Advice on How to Control Your Anger

Descrierea CIP a Bibliotecii Naţionale a României
J.M. BENNETT
HOW TO KEEP YOUR COOL. The Ultimate Guide to Anger Management, Discover Expert Tips and Advice on How to Control Your Anger / J.M. Bennett – Bucharest: Editura My Ebook, 2021
ISBN

J.M. BENNETT

HOW TO KEEP YOUR COOL

The Ultimate Guide to Anger Management, Discover Expert Tips and Advice on How to Control Your Anger

My Ebook Publishing House
Bucharest, 2021

TABLE OF CONTENTS

FOREWORD

Everybody has likely felt anger at one time or another. While particular individuals get angry more often than others and have regular, intense outbursts, others tend to bottle their feelings and then blow up or flare up without warning.

Anger is a basic human emotion and a natural response to situations beyond our control. There are a lot of things that may set off or contribute to anger, like the actions of another individual, an event, tension, expectations not being met, feeling hurt, contempt, humiliation, embarrassment, jealousy and sorrow.

Depending upon how it's dealt with and expressed, anger may be favorable or damaging. It has favorable effects when angry feelings help you address an issue or subject with yourself or a different individual and correct the situation.

Handling anger positively enables you to put damaging emotions into perspective. When you wish to let off steam, feel frustrated or distressed, there are constructive methods to channel your anger like listening to music or going to gym. These are frequently utilized in treating anger disorders.

But, expressing anger in a negative way frequently leads to assorted unhealthy behaviors like violence and aggression. You might get out of control and threatening to other people. When anger interferes with your power to think or act clearly, this may cause you to receive unnecessary trouble.

If anger cramps your personal relationships with friends and loved ones, leads to violence, makes trouble in your business life, or individuals fear your temper, you might be suffering from anger disorders and addressing anger becomes crucial.

The Secrets Of Anger Management

Learn how to control your rage and take control of your life.

Chapter 1

Basic Tips For Keeping Your Cool

Life certainly is unpredictable. You never know what may happen to you with each fresh day, for better or for worse. We cope with all sorts of individuals and with all sorts of states of affairs. Nevertheless, one thing is for certain – we do face individuals and states of affairs that annoy or anger us. Therefore, it's better to face the fact that we do become angry at times and to begin dealing with it for our own benefit.

Chill Out

Frequently in situations, we let individuals get to us. Make sure you evaluate if someone is purposefully attempting to make you angry. If this is the case, then there's all the more reason for you not to allow them get the gratification of driving you to your breaking point.

Maintain your cool! On the other hand, if somebody gets on your nerves without meaning to do so, you need to control this sort of anger as well, or you might wind up injuring someone for no apparent fault of theirs. Whenever this is the case, a friendly chat might be the solution.

Once anger appears as a consequence of direct provocation, it's commonly with an aim to get you into some kind of trouble. Don't let that occur. As an alternative, inhale and exhale calmly, and you'll clear your mind by doing so. The moment you fly into unrestrained rage, you've already lost the fight.

If you're the object of another person's anger, attempt and get yourself as well as him under the effect of composure, by speaking in a gentle tone. It's the natural feeling to shout at the other person, but try to quash that; you might resolve the state of affairs in a matter of seconds this way.

If you discover yourself in a trying state of affairs where you can't really display your anger, you may vent it into something innocuous like scrawling on a piece of paper. This works well particularly in places like formal encounters and business discussions. Physical exertion is a different good way to drop off some anger and get something constructive out of it in the deal.

Get in command of your anger and release it in doses when and if called for. If you're in charge, you need to let the individual in question recognize that he's angered you. This may be done in a number of ways, and different individuals need to be spoken to differently. Shouting is seldom ever the correct path, it only helps demolish relationships.

Lastly, when you've done something inappropriate yourself, do be truthful enough to admit the fact and to apologize where required – this far and away is the most crucial anger management technique.

Chapter 2

Anger Classes and Counseling

There are only a couple of individuals who may truthfully say they've their anger in check. A lot of us do fly into rages when the correct strings are pulled by others or by situations that come up every now and then. You don't have to have made a crucial error to register yourself in an anger management course or counseling. You need to do so prior to that happening. As it is sagely said, a stitch in time saves nine, and that's only too real with anger management. Take charge of your anger prior to you causing some severe damage.

Courses

Employers frequently arrange seminars and guest speeches on anger management, as they recognize that when tempers are in check, there will be a better work environment in the company. This is particularly true with jobs where deadlines are rigorous. Non-government organizations likewise arrange anger management classes every once in a while, most of which are free for all to go to. That’s a good place to begin if you're looking to get that anger in check.

Discovering the correct anger management course:

The net is a good place to start looking for the correct course in anger management. You'll likewise find a number of e-books and articles on the matter, a lot of which might be free to download. Most organizations will have their ads published online, and you may well find an anger management class in your city merely by looking online. If that doesn’t work out, try the yellow pages. The correct anger management class may be just a telephone call away.

Why you'd wish to enroll in such a course:

Well, the first reason is that it's going to help you live a more beneficial life. All the same, a few individuals would not want to accept that they require help, and the riskiest cases commonly fall into this class. It would be good for a trusted friend or family member to step in as counselor to such individuals.

Habitual abusers and recovering drug addicts are individuals who certainly need help with anger management. This is all the same not so simple at times. It's a hard task to convince somebody they require help when they don't wish to accept the fact. It's better to leave the counseling to the trained professional psychologists and counselors. It's adequate if you as a loved one or friend, could convince the individual in question, to get together with a professional.

When an individual is enrolled in an anger management class, that’s one-half the battle won right there. In simply a couple of sessions he or she recognizes they are getting in command of their emotions and consequently in control of their lives, and that’s not a sense that anybody disfavors.

Counseling

It's a myth that anger management counseling is for the odd deranged person alone. Anger may and does affect everyone, and it's true that it has a bigger effect on some individuals than on other people. All the same, if you don't learn to check this emotion, matters may take a turn for the worse any given day, and you may well discover it controlling you one day. It's consequently good for anybody to take a lesson in anger management.

The opening move is to understand what anger is all about. Ask yourself the critical question of whether you present a threat to yourself or to those around you when your anger finds you. If your reply is yes, then you need to look for professional help from an anger management counselor sooner than later. Do so prior to you causing damage to your life and perhaps to somebody else's likewise.

Realize the harmful effects anger may cause. It certainly is common to see individuals with unrestrained tempers. How frequently do we yell at the youngsters when they make errors, actual errors? It's alarming to see individuals striking out at creatures because they made a mess in the front room. After all, what else is to be anticipated from an untrained pet? The answer may never lie in violence, it does lie in conditioning. All the same, that might be veering away from our subject. In any event, if you recognize you act in such a way towards trivial events, you'd do well to get anger management counseling.

Unrestrained anger may spoil a perfectly great day at the slightest bit going wrong. When your anger irrupts, your muscles get tense, your facial gesture turns into a scowl, and this is broadly accompanied with verbal abuse. Not a very jolly sight you'll agree. If you suspect you might have an anger issue, do try to talk to a close relative or good acquaintance about it.

Get feedback on your anger. Is it unrestrained? May it pose a threat to you and to other people? The role of this individual in your life may do you the utmost good. Do take the feedback and utilize it to bring about a positive effect in your anger management. Of course, it would do no good if the only result of the person's feedback would be that you get bad-tempered with them.

Counseling will help you face your issue instead of hide behind a cloud of anger. You'll get to recognize your inner-self better, for better or worse. In any event, it will help you get to be more in tune with yourself and more at peace with yourself. The counseling procedure will sooner or later help you get in command of your emotional side, and consequently in control of your life likewise.

Chapter 3

Recommended Things To Do For Adults And Kids

A lot of individuals suffer fits of rage and anger and though most youngsters are the exception, at times older youngsters might be susceptible to feeling uncontrollably mad and lost too. Those that may identify with this issue of untamed anger are in a better situation to be helped as realizing the state of affairs is the first proactive step one may take towards joining up for anger management classes and utilizing ways learnt there to their everyday lives.

Methods

Aside from acquiring the chance to learn anger management processes at assorted stages in the courses, individuals get to learn ways to deal with confrontational spots under adept guidance of counselors and medical health specialists. Taking part in a assortment of anger management activities helps people that have trouble checking their temper and those disposed toward violent or rude behavior to give vent to their opinions in a less adverse, more favorable and ordered manner.

One of the diverse activities taught to people at anger management courses is to verbalize their angry feelings while still a different effective strategy is to free the angry emotions with exercise. This is a favored form of anger management technique as it has a positive mood heightening effect on the person, lessens negativity and is easy to follow; from walking or running in the park to working out or playing a sport, there's no shortage of choices for relieving steam - positively.

Additional healthy ways to re-direct the energy consumed by being angry include proceeding on a hike, communing with nature, being in surroundings that bode peace and beauty so as to enable the lowering of tension and worry that go hand in hand with surplus anger. The stress release furnished by exercise that's pleasurable lets an individual clear their head, particularly those that call for any form of physical activity outdoors in the calm, regenerating beauty of nature.

In addition to the above methods to manage anger, individuals suffering from severe and unmanageable bouts of anger may likewise avail the services of a support group, attend a camp or a retreat to defeat the difficulties they're having with grappling with their tempers. Benefits of doing so include getting the job out in the open, knowing there are other people like them and this in itself helps them recognize they're not alone in dealing with anger management, which is a true issue. Merely uttering their problem helps some individuals feel better and presents them hope to plough through a hard stage in life while for other people, the group support presents them encouragement and mental potency to deal with diverse issues and basal themes that agitate them.

If youngsters get uncontrollably angry and defiant, anger management methods may be necessary to enforce to help them deal with a situation that's overpowering for them: but as youngsters are impatient with counseling on one-to-one basis and group support, the most beneficial way for them to deal with angry spots is to involve them in fun and games. From coloring books to keep them gainfully absorbed to finding them fun-trips to go on and sports hobbies to adopt that will burn the extra energy the right way. There are a lot of anger management methods beyond taking them to the therapist's chair that are feasible.

Therefore, anger management for grownups and that for youngsters are 2 really different attacks to take in order to show good and positive results that are long-term in dealing with unreasonable anger; no measure of intimidation or force may help bring these matters to the right conclusion as much as patient listening and reason can.

Picking an anger management activity that's fun, intriguing and pleasurable for the person is the most beneficial way to keep them centered on completing it and getting the wanted results.

Chapter 4

Dealing With Stress

Being and remaining infuriated isn't a mature response and anger management helps individuals faced with acute anger to deal with an overpowering emotion in a favorable manner.

Therefore, while professionals involved with contriving and instructing anger management specify it to be a technique of addressing, describing and solving a tense state of affairs by getting down to the primary cause of anger, they likewise help people recognize how to downplay stress during nerve-racking conditions.

Addressing Tension

This is most feasible when individuals faced with anger issues recognize there is little to be derived by being angry and a lot more to be accomplished by being tranquil. Even when anger lessens, the issue remains and individuals with long-standing anger-issues need to comprehend this in order to realize and work on the matters that make them angry and learn how to curb their responses to situations and harsh individuals that endanger their mental welfare.

The beginning and most elementary way to avail anger management help is to open up and express angry emotions and feelings that bring anguish, tension and anxiety in an individual with a sympathizing acquaintance or loved ones as most angry individuals require a kind ear when dealing with hard situations.

A mature listener will help the angry individual comprehend the other individual's viewpoint without wounding their feelings and smooth over rough spots in a calm manner, but sharing the issue is crucial to getting the correct help.

Putting down angry sentiments or maintaining a journal is a different effective anger management tip that minimizes stress as rather than speaking angry emotions, one has put them to paper; at times, this technique is more beneficial than confrontation, which may bring conflict and rifts to further the problem if the individual involved is also hotheaded.

Writing down angry feelings likewise has the advantage of being a strategy that helps one make conclusions about trigger-factors that contributed to the person getting angry.

Upon contemplation at a later stage one is able to re-read the notes made and this supplies insightful information on reasons for anger and maybe a clue into the true cause of the disruptive situation.

Discovering a solution is easier then, as well.

Staying away from a tense state of affairs or going off on a vacation or even a walk (me-time) is a different way to cope with anger that cuts down stress and keeps a individual away from possibly detrimental (for mental health) spots in addition to giving them time to contemplate their actions and the incident.

Spiritual study, prayer, meditation, and stillness are additional processes to deal with anger that bring down tension levels and wash off the pressures of life; individuals may take these up who are at ease with being solitary and want to cause a positive change in their lives. They're also regarded as being a balm for broken spirits and corrective power for world-weary souls.

Remaining healthy and in shape, studying breathing and exercises, getting enough rest and communing with nature in addition to looking on the brighter side of life are a few other good ways to cope with anger and a lot of individuals find the answer in music as well as opposed to confrontational techniques. Choose the one that fits you!

Chapter 5

Accepting

The most crucial step in anger management is recognizing if you're easily aggravated and have an angry personality, and finding out how to take responsibility for your reactions to anger and aggravation.

Angry individuals live with elevated levels of frustration, but great anger management methods let them learn to keep their irritation in check, by accepting their disposition, and accepting the responsibility of coping with it, by studying anger management methods to deal with the prompts and triggers that may rapidly turn to anger.

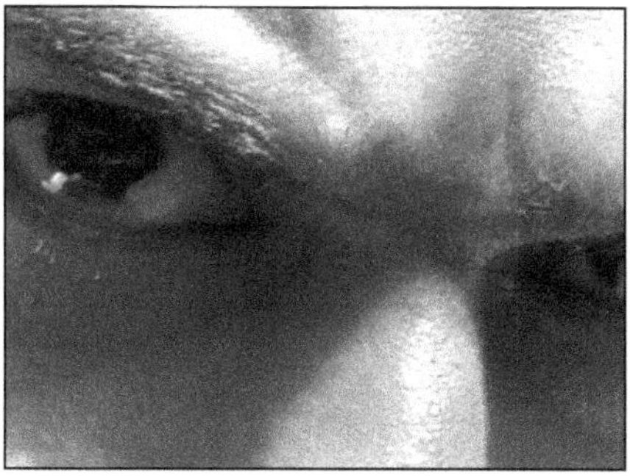

Admit

By exercising stress management methods on a regular basis, and utilizing physical exertion to work off their aggravation, they are able to realize the first signs of anger, and take a time out to calm down, minimizing the likelihood of discharging their anger on other people.

Mature individuals attempt to exercise positive ways to deal with their anger in a controversy. One favorable way to cope with anger against family is to make a contract that they may leave during a riff, whenever they feel that they may lose control. Just go to a private spot for break. Privately they perform damage control processes like waiting out the initial surge of the anger, and attempting to think from the other individual's point of view, to bring their anger level downward and then return to cope with the issue.

Admitting that you've an anger prone personality and realizing the need to actively work towards anger management in order to live a more pleased life, makes the difference in dealing with anger successfully.

A dedication to discipline and taking parenting classes to seek more efficient means of disciplining their youngsters, taking anger management classes, and taking part in couples counseling, helps angry people to learn more beneficial ways of being with the individuals they work and live with.

A few individuals with high degrees of frustration monitor themselves and work at bringing down their anger reactions, through positive anger management techniques; as their moral sense tells them that their flare-ups harm other people. A few individuals realize that they're acting out angry reactions they learned from their own parents, and sending that legacy down to their own youngsters. A few get assistance as their partner gives them the ultimatum of threatening to leave them if they don't get assistance.

Some get assistance only after they lose their mate and loved ones, but unhappily, a few never learn anger management techniques that may save their relationships, if not their own lives.

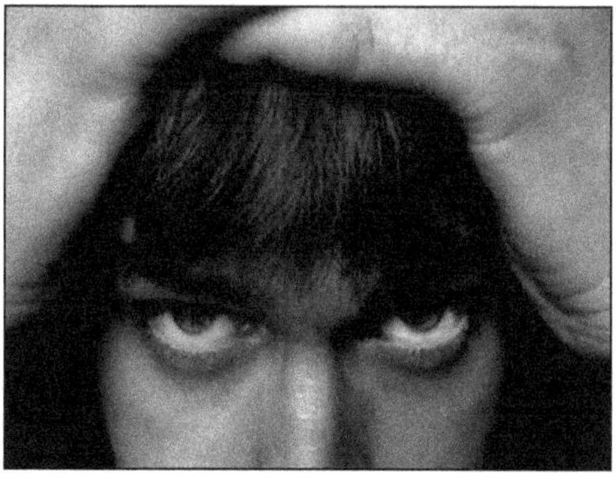

Chapter 6

Using Yoga

Anger is among those powerful emotions that tend to color everything in an individuals experience - it's like viewing the world through anything but rosy glasses. I've had my share of furious episodes, so I've seen first hand how anger may overcome you and inform every action you make. Yet discovering how destructive it may be truly hit me a few months ago.

A Good Technique

I was catching up with an acquaintance that I haven't seen in quite awhile. She'd been experiencing a harsh time for the past year. Her frustration over her marriage and her business life had been expanding for well over a year.

As she jabbered about what was occurring in her life and why everybody in it was causing her frustration, I took heed worried that one day all this rage would harm her health. She was already suffering from an assortment of physical symptoms that I'd bet was due to her emotional tension.

We were joined by an acquaintance who shared a story about a different individual being taken advantage of by a friend who ended up on the bad end of the karma caravan. My really angry acquaintance hurried to condemn the individual in the story - who she doesn't know - who committed the unfairness.

I was shocked by the hate in her voice, particularly considering she didn't even know the individuals in the story. It made me so really sorry to see how the anger spilling over in my acquaintance was morphing her into somebody that I didn't even recognize. Not only was she harming herself, but also she was harming those around her, including her three kids.

Fortunately, there are more constructive ways to deal with rage - yoga and breathing for instance. Here are a few drills to help you diffuse anger and prevent yourself from winding up overpowered by it:

Anger doesn't have to consume you from the inside. Instead of suppress it; try working it out with these exercises. Yoga includes physical postures, meditation and breath work or pranayama. Any of these factors may be utilized for anger management.

We will center on breath work. Pranayama is a common term to describe all yoga breathing drills. Prana stands for life force and yama means to direct it. Below are two different sorts of yoga breathing exercises that have been simplified to make them simpler and more practical to accomplish. Each pranayama may help you handle anger effectively.

Attempt this simple yoga breathing exercise to help you chase away anger. Breathe in through the nose and making a "ha" sound, breathe out the mouth and stick out your tongue. Duplicate two to three times. This lets your breathing get deeper and help release physical stress in the lungs and chest. This is a version of "lion's breath." It will just release the anger without drama or trauma.

Restart normal breathing by breathing in and breathing out through the nose. Without being forceful, take a couple of breaths where you pause somewhat at the top of the inhale and then exhale. If you feel dizzy or faint, stop the breath work and merely return to normal breathing.

Now, attempt to do several more rounds of the pausing breath work with somewhat longer breaks between the breathing in and breathing out. Inhale for a count of four, hesitate for a count of two and exhale for a count of four. Duplicate two more times. Stop the breath work if you get dizzy or you feel you're working beyond your lung's capacity.

If you experience any physical irritation, merely return to normal breathing.

You've completed breath work for day one. For the following thirty days, repeat the lion's breath and a simple three rounds of pausing breath work. As long as you're able to do the pausing breath work with no discomfort, persist in your routine.

Once you've comfortably practiced this breath work for at least a couple of days, put it to the test: the next time you sense you're going to lose your temper, take a lion's breath. Then, do the pausing breath work: breathe in for four, hesitate for two, breathe out for four.

Even doing this for one round will help you dislodge your anger long enough to intensify your breathing. Rehearsing this breathing exercise will help you learn to hesitate. When you're able to pause in a confrontational situation, you'll be more likely to be responsive, not reactive.

Chapter 7

Using Meditation

Meditation is more than a technique for relaxing the body, as some individuals think. It's a way for gaining freedom from ceaseless, nagging thoughts and cares, quieting the chatter of the brain, and attaining inner peace and happiness. In its greater levels, it leads to spiritual awakening, Nirvana, and to realizing who and what you are.

De-Stress

Though it plays a crucial role in assorted religions and spiritual practices, it's really a practice that's free from all religious intensions, and has forever been practiced everyplace, from ancient times until the current day.

There's always been the desire to go inside, to discover what is beyond the physical form, and to discover the true spirit and the relation between mankind, the world and the creator.

There are a lot of forms, techniques and traditions of meditation, which are rehearsed and followed for assorted reasons and aims, for relaxation and health, for mental mastery and inner peace, and naturally for arriving at spiritual awakening - Nirvana, and for discovering who you truly are.

Meditation calms the body and the brain, cuts back stress and anxiety, normalizes the blood pressure and has a curative effect on the body. It betters the power of concentration, focuses the brain and strengthens the intuition. Its steady practice reduces the number of uneasy thoughts in the brain and brings inner peace, felicity and bliss.

In order to get results it has to be practiced daily, at least once a day, twice a day is more beneficial. A beginner might start with simply ten minutes and gradually increment the time.

Basically, there are 2 sorts of meditation. One that calls for centering the brain on a particular activity, like on the breathing process, or on a concrete object, mental image, a word, idea or a quality of character.

The other sort requires that you don't center on any concrete object, thought or mental image, but to void the mind of thoughts, and blend into the inner silence within you, into your true, inner self. This sort may only be practiced after one is well trained with the first sort.

Below you'll find things you are able to do to better your ability to meditate, mitigate the inner resistance of the brain, and better your chances of success. Read them with attention, and apply them to any strategy that you practice.

Begin with an easy meditation strategy. Here are 2 examples:

Center your attention on your entering and outgoing breath.

- For a couple of moments, center your attention on your breath. Breathe normally, while centering on the act of breathing in and breathing out. Be heedful not to strain your breath and your body.

Centering on a motivating quote.

- Pick out an inspiring quote, and repeat it in your brain, attempting to find its deep meaning, on the far side of the written words.

Chapter 8

Talking To An Angry Person

When we talk to an angry individual, our verbal and nonverbal language helps to direct whether they intensify and get angrier or de- escalate and chill out. We hear too frequently in the news about individuals who were out of control and a crisis developed where individuals were hurt. We can't give ourselves any guarantees, however, we may put the odds in our favor and help to make certain everybody is safe. I'm going to give you the research based steps that are demonstrated to help when you speak to an angry individual.

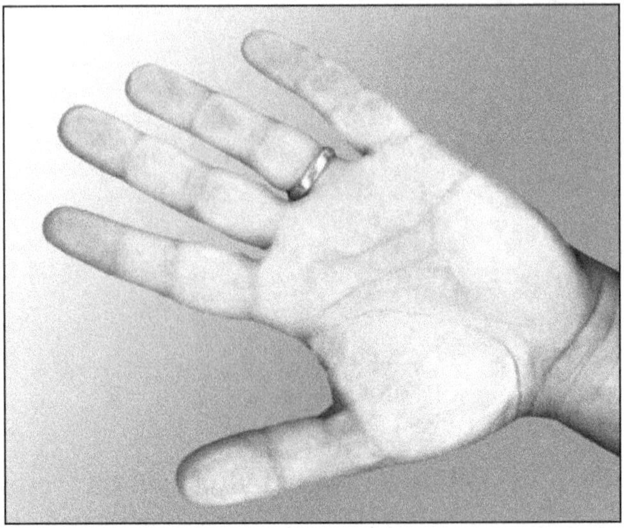

Calm The Situation

When you speak to an angry individual, remember how their brain and body will react. As anger intensifies, individuals tend to go into a fight or flight modality. When that occurs, their thought processes decelerate, but their sensory acuity step-ups.

They tend to perceive matters as closer, louder, larger, more menacing, etc. They likewise simply really wish to vent and to be heard, it's crucial that we keep these things in mind and utilize this knowledge to guide our own actions.

Be a great judge of when to acquire help. If you've the last bit of concern, make certain you're not alone and that you've an escape route. Individuals may sometimes intensify very fast. Don't try to handle an angry individual all alone.

If you speak to an angry person, it's always best to err on the side of care. These steps are not intended to imply that you may always talk somebody down and they're also not the only interventions. Utilize your own good judgment.

Mind gestural language. Remember the saying that actions speak louder than words? If you speak to an angry individual, give them extra physical space. Desist from talking with your hands. Don't lean towards them. Somebody being too close or hands moving may be sensed as threatening as this is an individual who's upset and is perhaps not thinking rationally.

Talk in a quiet, calm, pleasant tone and at a slower rate of speed. It's natural to mirror the emotions of the individuals we speak to.

However, if we mirror their emotion by elevating our voice or becoming upset then we have simply helped to step up a potentially dangerous situation. Lower your voice and mouth in a calmer, quieter tone and they'll be more apt to mirror you. Likewise, when individuals are upset, their comprehension tends to diminish. Talking slightly slower will help them to listen to what you're saying. When this occurs, you're guiding how the situation evolves and you're helping to prevent a crisis.

Hear them and validate their feelings. Frequently, individuals who are upset simply wish to be heard. The more they feel like individuals are not truly hearing them and addressing their needs, the louder they'll shout. Regrettably, there are times when they escalate to weapons or additional violence to be heard. Regardless what they're saying, listen. Giving them your undivided attention. Recognize their concerns. However, don't be judgmental! Don't state, "I can tell you're angry." Statements that label their feelings might tend to upset them even more. Rather, say "what I think I hear you saying is" or something similar.

React by verbally "disarming" them when you speak to an angry individual. Be amenable. What they truly wish is for somebody to hear them and to validate their feelings and make everything right once more. Say something that you're comfortable with that is a favorable response. This may be "I agree" or "you've a right to wantto exchange/get treatment " whatever they wish. If you see an individual escalating, let them know that you're going to try to get them the help they want.

Wrapping Up

Individuals of all ages certainly need help when it comes to commanding their anger. Accepting that you've an anger problem is the beginning next only to treatment and discovering how to cope with it.

The help you are able to get to cope with your anger effectively is by using techniques and strategies particularly tailored to take on anger. If you happen to be lucky enough you might even be able to do away with it for good. When you accept help in anger management, you'll be able to face and deal with any kind of situations effectively. You'd have likewise heard how react in assorted situations with composure.

3 of the basic responses, which many individuals face when presented with a stressful situation, are, either they

suppress their emotions, get defensive or they start to lash out. All these responses are not good to manage anger.

If feelings are suppressed, they tend to produce damaging consequences in individuals. It might seem to be fine but the issue will be still there. The individual ought to be prepared to cope with the situation causing anger otherwise it may turn out to be even worse. Suppressing emotions will lead to bitterness, which may be there for years. It's better to deal with the issue than to accept the bad feelings.

When assistance is taken to deal with anger management, it helps people to manage situations that may be challenging. Individuals with anger problems likewise go on the defensive. If they're confronted with spots that make them angry, they tend to respond quickly. These individuals tend to respond with bitterness, which may likewise bring about hostile responses from others. So going on the defensive isn't an ideal way to manage anger.

If help is taken in effective anger management it helps them to assess the situations instead of responding to them by being defensive. A lot of individuals likewise begin lashing out when they face situations, which induce anger.

Individuals who are serious about working on their anger may greatly benefit from effective anger management. There are a lot of helpful anger management methods available free for those who are interested from assorted sources.

Those who are in need of help should recognize what this may do for them. Anger management methods will be helpful only to those who admit responsibility for themselves and want to alter their ways.

When you use an anger management program you're on your way to discovering how to effectively control your anger and cope with difficult spots.

CPSIA information can be obtained
at www.ICGtesting.com
Printed in the USA
LVHW081255101122
732762LV00014B/972

9 785375 266336